THE NICK OF TIME

ALSO BY ROSMARIE WALDROP

POETRY

Gap Gardening: Selected Poems
Driven to Abstraction
Curves to the Apple
Splitting Image
Love, Like Pronouns
Blindsight
Reluctant Gravities
Split Infinites
Another Language: Selected Poems
A Key Into the Language of America
Lawn of Excluded Middle
Peculiar Motions
Shorter American Memory
The Reproduction of Profiles
Streets Enough to Welcome Snow
Differences for Four Hands
Nothing Has Changed
When They Have Senses
The Road Is Everywhere or Stop This Body
The Aggressive Ways of the Casual Stranger

WITH KEITH WALDROP

Keeping / the Window Open: Interviews,
    statements, alarms, excursions, ed.
    Ben Lerner
Ceci n'est pas Keith—Ceci n'est pas
    Rosmarie • Well Well Reulity

FICTION

A Form / of Taking / It All
The Hanky of Pippin's Daughter

ESSAY

Dissonance (If You Are Interested):
    Collected Essays
Lavish Absence: Recalling and Rereading
    Edmond Jabès
Against Language?

TRANSLATION

Under the Dome: Walks with Paul Celan
    by Jean Daive
The Up and Down of Feet: Poems
    1994–2010 by Elke Erb
Triste Tristan & Other Poems by Paol Keineg
End of the City Map by Farhad Schowghi

Almost 1 Book / Almost 1 Life by Elfriede
    Czurda
Language Death Night Outside by
    Peter Waterhouse
quisite moment by Anne Portugal
Dichten=No.10: 16 New (to American
    Readers) German Poets, with A. Duncan,
    T. Frazer, N. Grindell, C. Hawkey
Lingos I–IX by Ulf Stolterfoht
The Form of a City Changes Faster, Alas,
    Than the Human Heart by Jacques
    Roubaud, with Keith Waldrop
I My Feet: Poems & Constellations
    by Gerhard Rühm
Many Glove Compartments: Selected Poems
    by Oskar Pastior, with Harry Mathews
    and Christopher Middleton
Desire for a Beginning Dread of One Single
    End by Edmond Jabès
A Test of Solitude by Emmanuel Hocquard
Where Are We Now by Peter Waterhouse
With Each Clouded Peak by Friederike
    Mayröcker, with Harriett Watts
The Little Book of Unsuspected Subversion
    by Edmond Jabès
Mountains in Berlin: Selected Poems
    by Elke Erb
The Plurality of Worlds of Lewis
    by Jacques Roubaud
Heiligenanstalt by Friederike Mayröcker
A Foreigner Carrying in the Crook of His
    Arm a Tiny Book by Edmond Jabès
The Book of Margins by Edmond Jabès
Dawn by Joseph Guglielmi
Late Additions by Emmanuel Hocquard
From the Book to the Book by Edmond Jabès
The Book of Resemblances by Edmond Jabès
Some Thing Black by Jacques Roubaud
The Book of Shares by Edmond Jabès
The Book of Dialogue by Edmond Jabès
Collected Prose by Paul Celan
The Vienna Group: Six Major
    Austrian Poets, with Harriett Watts
The Book of Questions by Edmond Jabès
Bodies and Shadows by Peter Weiss

THE NICK OF TIME

Rosmarie Waldrop

A NEW DIRECTIONS PAPERBOOK ORIGINAL

Manufactured in the United States of America
First published as a New Directions Paperbook (NDP1509) in 2021

Library of Congress Cataloging-in-Publication Data
Names: Waldrop, Rosmarie, author.
Title: The nick of time / Rosmarie Waldrop.
Description: First edition. | New York, NY : New Directions Publishing, [2021]
Identifiers: LCCN 2021021178 | ISBN 9780811230537 (paperback ; acid-free paper) |
ISBN 9780811230537 (ebook)
Subjects: LCGFT: Poetry.
Classification: LCC PS3573.A4234 N53 2021 | DDC 811/.54—dc23
LC record available at https://lccn.loc.gov/2021021178

10 9 8 7 6 5 4 3 2 1

New Directions Books are published for James Laughlin
by New Directions Publishing Corporation
80 Eighth Avenue, NY 10011

ndbooks.com

for Keith, always

CONTENTS

THE SECOND HEMISPHERE OF TIME

ASYMMETRY

1

There is no evidence that we have a special sense. Of time. You don't think it's pressing as you sit on a sidewalk in Providence. And let your inner ear. Regulate your equilibrium. At the edge of your eye, a black cat wanders among legs. You watch swallows drift high in the breeze as if the force of gravity did not exist. And a shimmer of sun through branches deepens to a memory. Of waking in a small garden. Among buildings that no longer exist.

2

Summer arrives in a strawberry, sweet, juicy. As long as you feel its flesh on your tongue you're unaware how. One minute inches into the next. But how could you observe awareness anyway? Or, for that matter, a thought? It grows in you, not as a sensation. (Nor like a baby or tumor.) An experience that you can't hold on to. Any more than to the smell of lilac. Though it soothes emptiness.

3

You can heed the way shadows grow. In the afternoon. Whereas you can't focus on forgetting, say, my name. Not a sequence of discrete acts like brushing it off. Your teeth. Another process more elusive than light fading. Into mere spaciousness where you don't hear my voice. Pass through the air. Which you breathe unawares while your thoughts run. To coffee like an express on its tracks.

4

You call it instinct. That you want to make the word your 4th dimension. A way to pluck the now and keep it. From being gone almost before it *is*. To live in a continuous present, like the cat that rubs her chin along your leg. Or Gertrude Stein. Or like that distant waking. Into light made complex by cherry branches cutting across it. So many leaf edges. Spread as widely as the phenomena of thinking.

5

Only in time is there room enough to think, you say. And order another strawberry tart. But thinking (alas) does not happen in front of your eyes, with a clear horizon. It spreads its light. Like sun behind a cloud. From no visible point of origin. And at no moment does the question "do fish think" come up. For air. Which is cooling. Because it's late afternoon, and the shadows of houses are longer.

6

The shadows have a bluish cast. But the cat's fur radiates tremendous desire. And how can we see time as it is when we treat it like a thing? To spend or lose while trying to hold on? To its perpetual passing? Like the sheen on the Seekonk sweeping ducks and swans toward the Bay. While we cling to the bank and count on a yield of air. Meanwhile the senses grow dull. The environment erodes. And Edith Piaf sings *Je ne regrette rien*.

7

We don't (like the ancient Egyptians). Vary the length of the hour. By how much daylight there is to be divided by twelve. And though your mouth is full of pastry (hallelujah) words are not. A translation of something that was there before. Not as your tart is of berry, flour, eggs. You try to find the place inside you where words come into being, to wrest from them what one might get. From a relationship. Even in a foreign tongue. The cat in full possession keeps the pigeons at bay.

8

While our conversation flows on. (Along with planets, the Seekonk, and the meaning of words.) Physicists are making the most determined attempts to circumvent the asymmetry. Of past and future. Just as your mind does as it returns. To that overlay of intense light and leaf. In the garden of your childhood. Do you feel a sudden deepening of warmth? On your navel? Does it make you think of the word "love"?

9

A sentence with the word "time" in it already contains a shadow. Of the soul leaving the body. And at the word "leaving" a bird (or an insect?) rises. On a diagonal. Toward the flock of its feather. Seen darkly through the glass of otherworldly ideas. Just as again and again you think what we experience as time. Is only the outside. While hidden within the deer and the antelope play. Not to mention those vague creatures, our memories.

The antidote to such speculations might be a complete inventory. Of the things present in the present. Busses, cars, sun, pigeons, cat, table, spider, coffee cup, etc. But where then do we locate feeling? In our breast or facial muscles? In the gestures we make with our voice? (Like lucidity gathered from the surface of phenomena?) Or in that sunlight through the cherry tree that is etched into your brain? Though that small body is no longer possible. And of the garden nothing remains.

BITS AND PIECES

1

Bits and pieces, you say, scratching your beard. That's what there is. Stalks rising in the air as if gravity did not exist. Roots, dirt, turtles, elephants. Because the singular wastes territory we try to link it to galaxies or melting ice. For a coherent universe. But not dense enough to attract, mere pieces, always, just as they were. Is this why we have offspring? Why I say *my* hand, *my* foot, to make them more intimately felt than objects usually are in the mind? Can the withness of the body undo isolation?

2

This almost physical wanting of continuity, if possible, happiness. It makes us smooth over the gaps with a twist of muscle on a field of error. We call it instinct, and it spreads like a heatwave. Even to the distant mountain whose slopes seem softer for being beyond touch. But our ambitions contradict one another: you also love this particular patch of blue in the sky. You fear debris in the brain will bury this one insistent hydrangea that stands out from the sprawl of green. You say hydrangea. And again: hydrangea. As if the intensity of the word could keep the plant in bloom.

3

If memory serves, it was five years ago that yours began to refuse. Does it feel like crossing from an open field into the woods, the sunlight suddenly switched off? Or like a roof without edge or frame, pushed sideways in time? Like the flashes in which we think we possess though never quite reach ourselves? Yet today is today. And you receive it, if in pieces. Likewise words. If intermittently. Then you let them move over your tongue and hold their possible bodies in both hands.

4

It seemed almost personal when the sun was eclipsed. As if visibility were like your memory, or the moon's shadow the cataract on my eye. Observing the latter did not make it pass. Unlike when a fright resolves into the joy of not yet. I keep on standing as I've learned to, having feet. Though electrons degenerate and the knife-edge is moving closer. I treasure the residues of love's radiation, put on sneakers and wait for the form of rejection to come. Whether you'll no longer know my name or walk out of your body, I anticipate I'll swallow. As if it were a hard object.

5

Meanwhile you cling to your book. Do the words still float you to Prospero's island? Or drop, separate coins, bringing no dew from the Bermudas? I put my hope in the fundamental difference between local time and time at a distance. Make a show of clearly contoured identity, no matter if you can connect it to family structure. A stable body with only occasional modification. Rather than molecules and feelings in violent agitation. Let alone quanta dissolving into vibrations of light. You stare at your left little finger, which is crooked.

6

Veins visible under your skin, translucent. The first stage of a fare-thee-well? Cypress, pine, yew, taxus, the evergreen punctuation of our final sentence? Elsewhere, in territories off the map, does time warp, whirl, meander, fold, get trapped in wormholes? Careen into complexities of curves and lives we will not have? Here, the clocks are synchronized with dusty noise. And breath is short. I count the pulse pushing through my neck and try to match it to your breathing. The escape velocity of the unknown.

7

Perhaps if we had dark-adapted eyes. The shadows would not overtake us. And you could brush your teeth without fearing for their skin. Add the conjunction of being prudent, and night broader and deeper. Because you are still within it. Could this not disperse the threat? As in a mirror? Could it not offer the possibility that your illness, even if deliberate in its purpose, need not proceed in a straight line? Could slow in the gravitational drag of my body?

8

Am I trying to write my anxieties down into the deep of the paper? In such a way that I could draw them back inside me? Completely? This has nothing to do with poetry, but perpetuates denial and mental reservations. To my surprise you say: Even blind with incomprehension, we must. Trust the words we still have (with their tangled depths and roots) to house the world in the complex of our feeling. As if they could love us.

THE ALMOST AUDIBLE PASSING OF TIME

1

I've been sitting so still I might be part of the garden. Time might shut down if I weren't still cultivating an edge of desire. Its thirst, its burst toward the region of expectation. The way a hungry baby stretches its arms toward the mother's breast. Or the cat keeps eyeing the grackles black as if already night. A pale moon hangs ready for her cue, though shallow sunlight is still sinking through the air. The future. Surprising we can think of it, its uncertain contours, body, mass. When the ads all announce end-of-season sales.

2

The garden in fact lies behind me, is nothing but an act of memory. Along with the dry smell of a stone wall crumbling at the point where sky and earth would come together. All our temporal concepts can be traced, it is said, to feelings of effort and fatigue. Just as it takes learning and failure to become aware of our capacities. Encouraged, with luck, by a mother's smile. But can I look at a word as if I hadn't learned to read? Were still running through high grass, smelling the sluggish Main river mingled with distance, and the lilac purple? The day all dew and dawn, dusting sleep from birdwings? Even though your nose is in your book I can just see you roll your eyes at such silly questions.

3

Ritual, repetition, rhyme. For centuries we've tried to thwart the arrow. But even when, at the prayer of Joshua, the Sun stood still, time nevertheless continued. Likewise when Rousseau tossed his watch. Staring at the mottled bark of the sycamore, do I think this ritual will protect me from the constant changes of my body? The run toward dust to dust? Is it to freeze this moment before the mosquitos come with their cargo of itches that I watch beetles and weeds and pods, as if I were interested in them? But I don't even know their name—when words and their entanglements are my feelers. Without them I'm in darkness.

4

I search the cracks between my English and German for more words than either has. To gather gradations in softness of the late afternoon air. As if they could help my nerve impulses not to fire on the all-or-none principle like our elections, but to transmit even the slightest discrepancies of light, the weakest hum of an insect. But even though the leaves soften the edges of the tree the alphabet takes many American minutes to take the place of one look. And it's the pale moon between the leaves, not a symbol, that triggers the image of a German farm lost. In strata of time solar, sidereal, nuclear. Where the pale light stretched out the distance. And the cows chewed their cud so slowly—immeasurable by any clock. A different time, not suited to the ephemeral.

5

No matter what comes into the house, a letter, today's paper, you are convinced you have already seen it. As if your present were being devoured by an imposter past. Whereas I look at my hands and think I've never seen those veins. True, they are more prominent now. As if asking to be recognized. And the moon up in the afternoon. Perhaps the present is only the past gnawing its way into the future. So that our day does not exist at all. No, no, you say, it's simply over.

6

One day rolls into the next no matter how I wind myself up. Most of my time gets mislaid. Or returns as a bruise, counterclockwise, admitting its nature of calamity. Pain remains in the body even if the wasp is already far away. As shrapnel can lie dormant for years and yet give an old soldier gyp in damp weather. So it might be well to write down warnings. Even mislaid, time burns at both ends, and my body no longer moves with the energy of electrons through longitudes, latitudes. And in altitudes I get sick. My face tells the time without wheels or springs moving inside the brain.

7

Both the words *tempus* and *templum*, the carpenter's two crossing beams, signify intersection. Into geometry. Has time been drawn and quartered. This need not bring tears to your eyes, you say. Still, I'd rather, like the ancients, stick with the movement of the heavenly bodies. Cycles of sleep and waking. Birds migrating from cold region to warm. The rate of polar ice melting. Or the beat of iambs or the subtler pulse of prose.

8

The instant of late sun on my hands feels worth two birds out of reach. On which the cat's attention is riveted. My attention wanders. Not by hops and jumps, but alternate diffusion and concentration, like the foot of a snail. As if thinking were a method of scratching on these clumps of earth, and I could grab a fistful in order to hold on. The way I press words deep into the paper. Do I hope the breaks between them will interrupt, if not beat time? The way thinking of "the cows" enlarges this small plot into a plain? Because cows move slowly and in the distance?

9

Wittgenstein claims words are not essential. To what we call language. And it's true, in the tweets of birds much is meant and understood. But did he not recognize connective tissue? Even though he had skin covering his whole body? Of course, he also thought he could have a toothache without teeth. This opinion does not depend on the direction of time and so won't upset the flight of birds, you say. Nor keep the cat from contracting her pupils. To remove their picture?

10

I chase my little thoughts around a circle the way the cat chases her tail. Though more often she leaps into the nick of the kill. Once upon a time I spoke my mother's tongue, lake, pond, deep river, sea. And the wake of a ship showed not only the churn of water behind it, but the yet unrealized advance about to happen. Then, suddenly, I was an old woman, enveloped by evening cool. The waning light, damp on the skin, makes the yard less spacious, less direct than the remembered garden. I'm not a virtuoso of stillness like the cat, but feel the lightness born of fatigue. Of words that say nothing, but hang in the air like echoes. Or positive joy.

INTERVAL AND HIGH TIME

1

Americans, like the classical Greeks, are said to have short memories and little respect for tradition. Is this true? New buds sprout, green tufts dense with oblivion, but are the roots not steeped in old chronicles? And nowhere else have I found as many people researching family history. Hoping for generations of mothers, for sap to rise and nourish the self? You've sat years across from me, and the distance. Has not changed my feeling for you. Which fills it. It is possible, you say, that spacetime is finite but has no boundary. Has, as James Hutton said of the earth, no vestige of a beginning, and no prospect of an end.

2

Goethe thought the lack of tottering castles was America's advantage. The unencumbered "splendor of all *possible* experience." Of so many unborn tales that make the heart race in sleep. Through the leafy, limitless night. But what of the shiploads of withered ideas the pilgrims brought with them? That's why, you say, we must let our feet find their way. On a ground of emptiness. Must follow Goethe's *ich hab mein Sach auf nichts gestellt* and depend on nothing. As if one could.

3

Am I one of those immigrants who never discover America? Never truly arrive? Am I trying to reconstruct the places I left behind with French wine and books from Germany? Though words like raccoon, skunk, hickory, Narragansett, Pawtucket, and Pawcatuck. Have entered my vocabulary. Am I focused on the wake behind the boat that brought me rather than its destination? But you, though from heartland Kansas, are not all forward-looking either. You see a shimmer of sun on water. And don't go build a boat.

4

As long as we talk of the river of time, you say, we'll drown in its literal depth. And no explanation can pull us out. You, like your cat, won't go near water. Not even as a metaphor. And, despite their unequal weight, you're content to see time projected onto space, whether it's a point describing the circle of the clock face or the geometry of hyperspace. Meanwhile indiscriminate spring covers everything with tendrils and vines. A myriad insects hum, birds punctuate the luxuriant foliage. And I stumble, unaware of what's spreading underfoot. Including layers of feeling and the progress of stories.

5

The infrangible spacetime of the curved universe, you say blandly. How childish of us to try to adjust it to our measure, make it a human matter. But, I object, only while we exist is the cosmic arrow certain. To point in the same direction as the arrow of entropy. The arrow, you say, will kill itself. Words go from one breath to the next as if to drown time in an eternity of talk. Though sometimes swallows rise. Between the words. Whole flocks of birds whirled into the wind.

6

We claim we'd like to get out of the mechanical before and after. For what? A cycle where past and future are a matter of position? So that we could use one and the same word for yesterday and tomorrow? Or a focus on the now as in language, where time is always the time of the speaker? Or as in a painting, where the world stands motionless, holding its breath? But a whoosh of kids, two words in a row, and already we're tipped into interval and high time. I read my horoscope, which reaches well beyond the expectations of the season, while your mouth tastes of childhood and no tomorrow. But with a slight adjustment of perspective, longing, both forward and backward, can be cherished on its own terms.

7

To change our experience of time would be a real revolution. Would make our culture stretch sinews and joints, release unheard-of energies. The way, after a war, the patchwork maps float up in the air. With distinctions vanished as if painted all one blue by Yves Klein. Till we pull them back down and redraw the borders. Could time open and spill? Amorphous, without edge or direction? Like the portion of pure dark that goes unseen in every film? We'd be lost, eyes not trained to see paths on the face of the deep.

8

The way the sun moves time through leaves is less mysterious than the way time moves through us. At ever increasing speed. Toward the end of our lives, it is said, our beginnings return with freshly fluffed green, crocuses, robins, and orioles. As though we had sailed all the way around the clock, and I were making mud pies and didn't know you. But perhaps I've always misunderstood my feeling for you as knowing. And only realize it now as we move toward the smell of diapers. And memory. Is carried off into the dark. For now, though, bursts of sun redshift the mind. Spring is still legible, with all its atmospheric negotiations. And the smell of lilac heady.

LAMENT

THE POEM BEGINS IN SILENCE

Barbara Guest, 1920–2006

Where language stops matter begins. Of words. The simple contact with a wooden spoon. I don't easily give up on the uncertainties that might, if only for a moment, alleviate grief. But time is perishable. I believe. A sense of consciousness comes precisely. From the flow of perceptions. Relations of warfare and polka dots. And you cannot twice capture the flash of identity between subject and object.

The poem begins in silence, you wrote, mystery, wild gardens, pitch within the ear, chalk, rivulets, shifting persona, shuffling light.

As long as we've not reached, as in a dream, the fibrous, woody substance of words. We are prisoners. Of narratives in the room. Sprawling to consider an emphasis falls. On reality. Neither thick lids nor vowels inclement can obstruct the transparency of the dragonfly's wings. While the brain establishes consciousness through stimuli occurring not more than a twenty-fourth of a second apart. You occupy the lotus position.

The poem is fragile, you wrote, the contour elusive, ropes sway, heavy violets, galactic rhythm, sibilants, solitude edged, upward from the neck, provokes night.

When approaching death we cannot go into the matter of darkness. Viewed on the screen of distance, your shadow rephrased. Forbids the instant disclosure. The necessary night entangled in the folds of pre-occupation until the next bold seizure of dawn. It is the connecting between moments—not the moments themselves—that is conscious-ness. Field broken by low running water, dour sky, the earth in twists moving like the water into the body's memory of self.

The poem is a résumé, you wrote, of impalpable vision, the clair-obscur of thought, a brown mouse, twilight soup, the figure appears, adoptive day, scorched tongue, the edge, always.

After your death we find matter. For many fine tales about your life. And work. The speculative use of minerals, like beryl, to prevent attach-ment to words from overflowing. To catch the fraction of a second when the seam of present and future is visible in the flash of the lizard's flight. Loss requires restructuring all of our consciousness, our relation to sunrise. And giving way to the emotions.

The poem draws blood, you wrote, kicks away the ladder, rose marble table, folds of skin, mirrors, fans, nimble wind, multiplied by frost, the rage of night.

VELOCITY BUT NO LOCATION

1

Thought flies above the world and leaves it naked to the waist. Treetops bare but for nests of mistletoe, records stored in their DNA. There's no escape, you say, from the matter of fact, insistent, particular. Knife, leaf, bud, feather, hair, shell. If you cannot distinguish between trees, no use wishing it were winter, sea in front of your eyes, wind blowing. The doors of sense perception may droop no matter what there is to see. The environment introduces notions of more or less, trough or swell, cells suspended in undefined middle age. Where the unending rain falls on a group of chickens, that is where the color is.

2

With transcendent assertiveness our concept of spirit poses, denying its tie to reference standards in the brain and its frailty. But where should we point to show the mind is in pain? Assertive mess. Can we compare it to pushing the blanket down to our navel? a summer day? phenomenal cleavage? How ghostly the past, daring us to break its barrier. Yet insists that nothing we do is without connection to our embryonic development. Would a small vagina be a sign of refinement, like having no appetite? Or more like red pants seen across the expanse of the Rhine?

3

What, moreover, could break the horizon better than making love in a train, a moviehouse, the Egyptian section of the Met? The meaning of a word incorporates the world into our language. A trace of light from a distance, bruised edges, promise of orgasm, on tiptoe across the floor like a child's winged wonder, or hopping on one leg, a change of opinion, a new day. We have our plan and hold it open to its possibilities. But perspective means gradation of importance, of feelings about the infinitude of dots in the matrix, the matter. The way aging sharpens traits that in childhood were blurred by potential and the softness of young skin. Light implies shadows. And yes, on the page this word, trace, scar.

4

Hammocks suspended, these language games, without mosquito netting. Able to be fitted, to become, be used, or the like. There's no interest in a vacuum. Or mere agitation of things agitated. Bomb, threat, tract, wiretap. Worlds built and unbuilt, kept in motion when we should wince away from certainty that's nothing but a tone of voice. Talking in my sleep, a dream of the dark, the brain's own language, I don't sense the wood about to break, the shock of frailty, the storm, the crash. Is it raining? Then there's the illusion that syllables can be repaired.

5

A fact is supposed to be taken into my consciousness as if conjugating the verb "to know." Rather than like a lover to my bed, begetting concepts and turns of phrase as a lure for feeling. You can't just follow your hypothalamus, you say. But living beings are composed of the same constituents as the rest of the earth. Beans, barley, menhirs, dolmen, cairns. And my hurts are as constant and trivial as Lyn Hejinian's.

6

Even hardened propositions may backslide into a state of flux, the riverbed of thought shiver and shift, blood speed up its rhythm toward unknown ports, exotic languages, heifers grazing on bouquets of spring. I thought I could distinguish between the surge of blood and hope raked up like leaves. The word peace repeated as a mantra. But unsure where my body begins and external nature ends, I must act without a script, without clue which cue to heed. The plot falls apart, the ground's uncertain, nothing lasts long enough for its pattern to repeat, like wallpaper, for identification.

7

As if it were the definition of coherence: where there's uncertainty it will extend to the very roots, walls, alleyways, and flights of stairs. Frescoes on the facades try to disguise their crumbling, their weight enough to make the river flood. The noise bubbles through your sleep, in spurts, under the bed, over awkwardly held breath. Mouth, molar, cheeks, chair, chest. Is it enough to turn your eyes inward to catch the elusive creature in the mirror? to reassure yourself that you are human? Or does it take arms against deficiencies of language? Yet the uncertain is discovery's element, just as an airplane must leave the observable ground and take off into thin air.

8

Did I get my picture of the world by diagnosis? dreaming it on the scale of my body? swinging my arms in rhythm with my legs, as if this could give birth to harmony in information transfer? It is my inherited bruise against which I distinguish between tool and farce, hurts and kisses. Meanwhile science remains fascinated with formal relations. This allows fact to masquerade as reality while rampant April slips through the meshes of the net, and suddenly we need umbrellas.

9

Rather than on hard rock I should bank on sand that's now in one place now in another and so leavens the landscape. A theater of change. Even after our death, nails and hair keep growing, bravely, blindly. Dream roots and branches. I let gypsies read my future and don't entertain the alternative. Just as I take for granted the complex information carried by my cells. And sleepwalk as if I had already solved the riddle, smoothed the blanket, crossed the river. As if a night could last years, a party go on forever.

10

There are convictions anchored so deep inside me that I cannot set sail for other islands, of which there are many. As if I could not put my legs into boots. As if nerve ends had been amputated. As if all I could do is moan. Animals got a grip on the world. Scent. Consent. Economy of reflex. I'm less interested in digestion or other issues of survival than distracted by gleams of sunlight on a leaf. Linden, aspen, will-o-the-wisp or other details that wander on like extras on the set. And me still with the same cup of coffee, obeying signals from some ancestral traffic jam.

11

I may not be sure of the meaning of a word but I don't doubt it has one. The way I seem to see the ground with my feet, even the uneven ground in the garden, even when it's too dark to point a finger at the trees, every one of which will outlive me. The way I am sure of my body, but don't trust my feel for its edges enough to relieve myself like a man, standing, legs spread above the waterfall. Instead just fight against sleep, lack of stamina, the storm, such bitter cold, my fingers numb with. All the while trying to catch up with the words that outrun my understanding, let alone salt on their tail.

12

A thought is a tremendous excitement. Like a stone thrown into a pond it disturbs the whole of our double nature, bass, reed, breasted, boiler, *gänger*, entry folded over understudy doubling the cape of good dope. Even though each nerve fiber carries only one sort of signal and has to act together with others. The word *together*, however, and the little word *and* are nests of ambiguity. This is why you look for a device to measure how far we're out of each other's depth. Or bed. Intimate brace of nerve cells not all alike, immense number of words in infinite combinations.

13

for Denise Riley

There is pleasure in composition, in grasping the connection of the one and the many. The way we gradually discover how the dancer's movements are anchored in, and anchor, the axis she spins around, the way the backbone is held up by the muscles acting in concert; or our sense of self, by the mirror. Without it we are forced into constant activity to make up for the lacking image. Like the squid or dogfish, being heavier than water, must swim continually throughout their lives. Desperate activity, I say, and often fruitless, all brains incessantly active, down into our dreams, leaves off the fever tree, electric.

14

It's difficult to realize the groundlessness of our beliefs, but my style is fragmentary in any case, and my life as perplexed as my writing. Wrong connection, conniption, conclusion, shirt inside out, buttoned wrong, short breath. Rain comes, and mist clots about the trees. I reshoulder the wrong assumptions, say "I know" the way we'd say "I am in pain" and don't question evidence or self. But then, clear conscious discrimination is an accident between the vapors of the mind and the opaque body, the cracking of knuckles, biting of fingernails. Still, I believe that all mammals, apart from the duckbilled platypus and the porcupine anteater, give birth to live young, and the females nurse them.

15

At some point the temperature drops to frustration, powdery snow swallowing all sounds, tires, boots, and explanations. Then we have to pass to mere description and admit our secret affinity with confusion, which is as fundamental as order even though all living things labor to maintain the latter. No crystal ball or balm for the sorrows of reason. Which means treasure or treason depending on the conversation you have your foot in, and water, water. Meanwhile a man enters a bar, another goes by in the street, a woman looks in the mirror, a cat hisses at a cat, and a fly buzzes on the window pane.

THIRD PERSON SINGULAR

1

Language the condition, not only of transmission. Without its frame nothing but vague volition. Vision? Window? In the story, she's been out in the rain. Strains in vain to see a bit of blue blown cloudless, to line up fovea and love. Or does she covet the neighbor's garden with the maple swaying, making the space move? Not trying to focus a spotlight on sentence structure as you would, but like a child simply taking in the forms in front of her eyes. No matter if words or the clutter of the physical world. No matter if it lessens alpha waves and sense of self.

2

It is possible for both space and time to be finite without any edges or boundaries, but not for language to be without speaker. Air turbulence at teeth and lips. Bone. Ivory. Flesh. Shakes her wet head. Does not often hold her dreams up for scrutiny: to be a femme fatale? to have your name imprinted in her body? Babies as young as one month are more responsive to the sounds of speech than to any others. This does not explain how we develop the uncertainties of "if" and "though." Or the emotional balance that makes a paragraph.

3

Three persons in the verb. One speaks, one's spoken to, one, as the Arabs say, is absent. Groom awaited by the bride? Death, by the widow? Knows she must curb her eyes from touching you if she wants to take in anything else. In vision, as in language, much depends on interpretation. A tree trunk as a lover. A statue as something to point at. So that, at least in German, it will have meaning. The mass of the sun bends spacetime in such a way that, although the earth follows a straight path in the four dimensions, it appears to curve along a circular orbit of three-dimensional, saturated feeling.

4

The pouring-down rain, the pouring-down rain. Says it over and over, as if to drain the words from the system they are part of. Warm refrain to make her a first person, if only temporarily. Children born blind say "I" only after they've learned to play with a doll. Meanwhile turns in little quarter turns to dry herself. Almost a waltz. A reel. Smile. The arrangement of auditory pathways in the brain is similar to those for vision, not moving in a straight line at the same speed. Stampede. More like thinking philosophically, branching perspective into balconies swinging out over the void.

5

Of course one has to think. For thinking, categories are a help. Less so than the forty phonemes of the English language, especially when in local ink, pronounced with the entire face. Stands in front of the fireplace, blinking. Legs wide apart. The acquisition of personal pronouns is connected with the capacity for symbolic representation in which vision plays a central part. But how slow she always is to wake her eyes to the light while galaxies are moving apart everywhere. Then notices your erection and feels her good morning link to a deeper space inside her.

6

"I" says the speaker, the subject. I oppose thumb and index to invite you into discourse, my reality. And yours. She, the third person, is barred from speaking for herself. A pleasure almost like eating and drinking. Or love, for which the Oxford English Dictionary has no less than 24 columns of definitions. They neutralize emotion by "see above," spilled semen, no point scored. Stored. Reward. We might think that meaning fixes a word's place in the language, as anatomy or skin color that of a person in the house or back of the bus, but relativity has put an end to absolutes of space and time. Still, we can compare parts of speech with lines on a map that have a different function each: frontiers, roads, rivers, meridians, merriment. This is almost as exciting as grammar.

7

Not a substance whose molecules you could rearrange, the units of language can be defined only by their relation—to hours after midnight, snowfall, genitals? Lies down on top of the newspaper, which is arranged in columns like the nerve cells in the folds of the cortex. Noun. Frown. Her own. The retina detects rather than suspects, traces a series of small details to report to the brain. If she's told enough yarns, she wonders, could she reknit ties to the child's ability to drink in the new? Which she yearns for. No matter where. But especially in the emotional landscape where she measures time by how often she gives in to blind kiss-compulsion.

8

The third person remains beyond the threshold while I and you resemble each other. This makes her wonder: Is she really a person? And if no person, what? Touches the printed page as a talisman, as if its precise reference could teach her to be acknowledged by your stare even when the maple, the rain, the street, the park, all turn absent. What of the hypothalamus, seat of happiness? Do we need to name it, the way the child in her first year needs to attach a name to at least one person? Time runs more slowly near a massive body like your mother, its gravitational effect. She tells you to put the words where they belong. Then you'll possess something and incidentally yourself.

9

The third person, because not a person, can respectfully address majesty as easily as annihilate you. Is she mere interval? Between presence and present? Then time itself would be in pieces. No middle between shards of a singularity where theory's broken down. As when the eyes are prevented from moving, the signals fade within a second, and no picture can be seen. This frustrates the brain's program to seek out human features. There are other means of contact, she might say. Like touching hands, cheek, earlobe, neck, breasts, lips, genitals. The tame turtle too rubs against the threshold. Though even touch can be mistaken, and explanations drop into black holes or other contingencies.

10

So what is hidden in her stillness? No lexical entity nor particular individual. The third person pronoun is of anything. Impersonal inflection with distance very near. In species such as sheep or horses, imprinting occurs right after birth; in humans only as they develop the capacity to discriminate. Between face and price, cat and female sex, spilled seed and safari. Not yet between recognizing a sign and understanding a statement. The echo in her head is not of the big bang, but of sounds most likely to combine into a phoneme, the baby's exercise in the theory of probability. It has opened up a space that gravity can't bend in on itself. Where she can take in your words and carry them to term.

LAMENT

Robert Creeley, 1926–2005

Since time withdrew from your body we can see your mind as sheer expanse. Like a country read about, seen from a distance, visited. It's without borders, nothingness making inroads. It contains the sun and the nothing new under it. There is nothing it is, nothing not. Its way is into form, as the body's was out of the room, the door, the hat, the chair, the fact. It remains. And yet we mourn the end of a world.

IN PIECES

*Words
are
pleasure.
All
words.*
—Robert Creeley

NATURAL

Though not real like thought or possibility. The pattern of my reading, beginning with "there was," moves into the present. Like lifting a hand unsure whether to imitate duration or mimic passage. As long as form is never less than activity it's not *how* the cookie crumbles, but simply that it falls apart. Happenstance. A hat. A window. Whirling leaves. Why not trust the rest will follow? In the dream I could not see you because you thought you were hanging from a trapeze.

TONE DEEP

No sound is less than a sound or more. But music keeps us from hearing each one by itself. Says John Cage. It is a pity. No mother tongue unless a mother. Or many books demanding we enter their superb monotony. What tongue would not allow us to say *you* in the deep sense, intimate? Years of melancholy, errors in pronunciation. Something in the middle slows down. So many times a day I do not speak any language.

SO SLIGHT A SOUND

It doesn't make you dream, only pause painting your lips. And nothing follows. Not from. Steps gone past, message not understood. A fearful clarity dissolves whatever you thought you knew. House set back from the street. Open windows let the clouds enter. The brain complicates matters. Tell me. Tell me.

PLUGS AND SOCKETS

No recipe for poetry or sex. Just water. In panic you invent the crawl and hope for nine lives. Wives. What if your rhythm doesn't match any language? Runs down before reaching the knot in the wave? The hand is quicker than the eye, but space twists. The sun sets in the middle of a word. Then we don't know what's up. Or down.

ENCOUNTER

What could I think to say in local gestures? Slow into form and cannot catch the next. A zoo in the middle of the sentence? Sponge, antenna, wall, bomb? This time of life, to learn to talk to you. To sit down, a square character. To believe with words. Widening rings in the water. Or else clouds. In the sky.

To feel an idea is difficult. And rare. A private fluency of figment and frontier. A splinter in the sky. Let's not get sentimantic. The word "reality" is a word. Atoms are unpredictable, a warp in a continuous field, a gamble against the powers of disorder. But grammar can unpack a sentence it has taken you so long to understate. What open window? What thin but penetrating light?

BROOM OR HEATHER

Don't overestimate muscles. Or get on Hegel's high horse either. There is no end to the potential for disorder, but that's no reason to idealize definition. What is a bedpost? The bedpost, says Creeley, is an extraordinary shape. Between you and me and. When even the laws of physics are only probable, could going West prove you are young? And are you? Manifest desire. Is uneasiness?

THIS DELAY

It bothers you. Screen plus concepts is madness? Waiting for virtual black and white, systems of winter, knives dropping. You think I am beside myself. And after a time you are. Searching for oral forms in a culture of writing. Remember Homer had no general terms for "mind" or "body." The face at face value. Leaf blown by the wind. Changing color against the evening sky.

PERSEVERANCE

Not going anywhere. The overlapping of successive perceptions in the cortex. Texture of same and long. Or a kind of seeing wide enough to include being, power, knowledge, will. Hips at a tilt. A face hidden behind its choices. A finger pointing. A package to be untied. In the dream the racing hooves raised clouds of dust, says Kafka, flew over obstacles so fast I almost could believe in love.

UNDIVIDED ATTENUATION

Everything inside everything. A sparrow, a scarecrow, a snowman. In the mind. In time, in Providence. In search of. There are no more secrets, but I too have my center of gravity. And the void that I encounter may feel like something's passage. Through local air. Wintry. Clear.

Can it be found? Not here. No "small, local containments": galactic spin, wormholes and bridges, clotted cosmic cream. Large fields of indistinguishable details, peculiar motions in the brain. Don't ignore the whirling leaves. Where did I put my keys? Dark matter passes through us swallowing what little light. Amazed we are still talking. Still learning to. And we thought it was later.

ANY SINGLE THING

Is so complicated we can only give it a little shove with the knee. The cry of the gulls. The line between water and grammar. Horizon and interpretation. Between two blues. Field of error. My gestures not my own. Desire not a color. And the sound of the sea. Listen.

OFFERS OF SKY

Even a slight curvature in the path of the light will produce dim shapes of possibles. Night minus tears. Or where. The shared adventure. Or amaranth, love-lies-ableeding. Who sings this song? Who talks desire? And shortcomings as long as. High in the air. Or clouds.

THE EQUATION MUST BE BEAUTIFUL

Allow the first look its density. Before what words make of it. Or often, gusts of wind. Light compact in comparison. With what? Inert reason? But I admit that everything is interrelated. On the model of language. The lovers on the park bench, the bakery, the shadows playing on the wall. Breath quenched in multiple directions.

PRECONCEPTIONS WITHOUT DELAY

Because light finds a place to fall. If intermittent. I can live in a small word and lose my head for another. Despite the slowness of my work. I've not explained, at best described in more elaborate terms. Opaque. Opaque, the space of hesitation, ricochet of recto verso. But the kiss. Is admirable, simple syntax, easy tale. Mouth undone at the lips.

All the bodies, one by one, the measure. Says Robert Creeley. Composite, containing simples, as surely as words are pleasure. The door, the white door, all the doors. To the small range of wavelengths called the visible world. We've attached names. So I could speak to you. Now something in the middle has come apart. The word "I" sits on my shoulders. Ready for carnage.

LAMENT

A COMPLICATION OF GRAVITY

Anne-Marie Albiach, 1937–2012

My book is the fall of a body, you said. Yours, fragile, premeditated. Into the depth of the page, where mysteries might still speak. And time passes with infinite resources of slowness and is its own project of erasure.

Arrived none too late, you wrote, scar-tissued darkness, form as opposed to character, point, knife, displace the menace.

Headlong your rush, thoughts, desires in violent agitation, a heatwave. Then grounded, the flying carpet, prey to grammatical elements, fire sustained by adverbs and conjunctions. Intensity within the darkest howl of pain. Your horizontal position did not project nocturnal ease onto the day.

Can't without sensuality, you wrote, pedigree of thirst, desire of words for one another, vertigo, speed of chance, pure pulse free of cause.

Time has fallen into the hands of mathematicians, and clocks pretend to be synchronized. Hence your words in geometries across the gravitational fields and spilled metaphor. To give birth to an order of a different kind. Where even fallen among the nakedness of letters you might remain a subject. With clothes marking the boundaries of body by surrounding it and stimulating respiration.

Those women, you wrote, the lyricism of precision, dazzled by data, the wrist, upwrench, the splendor of syntax, complicit to the point of injury, they will come no more.

Though you opened all your senses to encounter you could not decipher the vast hostility of the real. In the mirror large eyes, but not yourself. You fled, hoping for ecstasy and full harmony with death. Then hesitated on the threshold to gauge the distance from body to text. This mystery, never fully resolved, has devoured you.

Uncertain dream, you wrote, the body as text, irreproachable absence, the scent of the rose, invisible from lack of self, song blazing incantescence, hair swept into the night.

MANDARIN PRIMER

ASPIRATES

Tea, coffee, or cocoa, which all arrived in London in the year 1652, are needed for serious study, its repeatable steps. Plus a primer from 1911. Most important: know what you want, for discovering the Far East of the self may require restructuring your world. It's a peculiarity of the genteel classes in both East and West to express surprise, horror, or other emotions, but rarely any precise thought. Whereas a pink raincoat is an antidote to stuttering "pudding please" when trying to voice aspirates. Their presence or absence makes as much difference to the meaning of a Chinese word as caffeine, a socially acceptable stimulant, does to tea. The Chinese, strange to say, coined the phrase "to send forth breath" to compensate for excessive distance in late afternoon.

TONES

A rhythmical chime, a musical imperative not unpleasant to the ear, unlike the West's belief that it is superior and naturally meant for global leadership. No sentence should be committed to memory without letting the upper even tone run in the track of shared perception rather than carefully guarded nautical secrets. Even if you reject the all-embracing determinism of magic you must address every object because there is truth in all things. Nevertheless you should not hold out one hand without keeping the other in reserve. The refinement of the rising and falling tones can change a love whisper into statistics and explains our concern for microadjustment. There was no technology known to Renaissance Italy which the Chinese had not developed earlier. See table on page 99.

PRONUNCIATION

P as in *park*, not bark.

Ch as in *church*, not jerk.

G as in *gunpowder* invented for use in fireworks, not cunning.

H has two sounds, one as in English *how* come the Chinese rejected the use of their invention for violent purposes, the other to be assembled from memory.

Sh is pronounced with the teeth closed and a damp cloth.

Hs, on the contrary, with the whole face.

Whatever the reason, because the Orient denied itself the use of gunpowder for violence it laid itself open to defeat by the Western barbarians.

Placed at the hub of language, they draw sap from ground and ancestors to nourish the phrases placed on sheets of paper, matching matter to manner. Complete unto itself, its soul vibrating to one single sound, China turned its back on the world during the 15th century. Alas for the vertigo of encounter, alas for our variants of causality, for we too are in this world if under blankets of heavy snow. There are 214 roots in the Chinese language as against 240 species of the *theaceae* family, of which only the bushy and rangy types make the best tea. See *camellia sinensis*. The radicals form part of every character. They are arranged according to the number of strokes and speed of thought.

VOCABULARY

A foreign language may be likened to a poem that at first seems in cipher, yet is all open and offered to you: *Chieh*—a verse, a joint, a holiday, a festival. *Huei*—a time, a Mohammedan. *Tien*—a point, an hour, a little, to punctuate, to light a lamp, to count, to test a hypothesis against the force of long rain. *Iong*—to use, need, require, take with, as in he cut it with a knife, a grain of salt. *Huan*—to change tea into foreign gold and silver, never paper. It is essential to master the monetary system because passing from one language to another is an operation of conversion and exchange.

CHARACTERS

A new character is often an old radical with a phonetic *je ne regrette rien*. While Europeans use the telescope to propagate their religion, the Chinese consider wisdom a combination of wind and lightning. The realities of life at sea and the unknown nature of the lands the Western explorers visited created a new, skeptical race of men that followed the rules of expediency. But what happens when the man is always upright, and the woman always sitting, with bound feet? The nerve cells never come to rest, showing that repose is not essential for basic nervous functions. Yet in a world without elsewhere, like ours, would Marco Polo leave Venice or sit in a well and look at the sky? Or study languages?

USAGE

Five years, four months and three days ago he gave me excellent cups three. Note the difference between "cups three" and English "three cups," mirror image reversing time's arrow. Thinking admits of turns as of degrees but can degenerate to a hum which is less even than remembering. The correct way of saying "less than" is "not to arrive at." A huge Western industry sprang up importing tea from halfway across the world, and for almost two centuries no one knew how it was grown or prepared. The he-bought things, cf. "the never-to-be-forgotten day," were not ten thousand perfections. It is an essential of good manners to ask a person's honorable name and age. My unworthy name is Chang, I have failed in business and wish to wash my feet.

ADVERSATIVE CONJUNCTIONS

Such is the force of the word "but" that the conclusion we would naturally draw does not follow. It is "turned upside down." Distinguishing between the contingent and the necessary, China banned opium in 1729. The British nevertheless exported 60 tons there from India in 1776 and five times that quantity in 1790. Ask how it got there, and all the world's a vessel. Hence the verb *hsiao-teh*, "to know" is heard more in the South than in the North. But "to beget" is the equivalent of "gentleman," used as a title of respect and stored in a cool, dry place.

CALLIGRAPHY

The laws of nature are large average effects which reign impersonally. Whereas the hand amorously caresses every single stroke, remembering the six graphic principles and the laws of revelation and concealment. So petals fall in the fountain and their pollen clings. Stone, bone, parchment, paper, screen. More and more fragile the support, the trace fainter and fainter and finally lost to a new generation of software. Yesterday it blew a great wind. The master's characters touch the four seas in one blink of the eye because he considers the nothingness at the origin and heart of everything.

The English drank many cups of tea or, as the Chinese say, not a few. In 1801 for example, two and a half pounds per head. Male and female come every day. But the Chinese who cross the sea to the distant near become shadows thrown too far from their source. There are two levels of scientific thought, one adapted to perception and imagination, the other beveled away from colors shifting in the sky. "Take this foreign garment to Mr. Ch'ien" is constructed as "take to Mr. Ch'ien there go." And the same spirit that permitted astronomers to reject the view that the sun rotates around the earth also made seamen skeptical of land-based authority.

RECAPITULATION

The word *tu*, "all," follows the noun and, like a clerk, takes complete inventory. Preceding a negative it gives you a turn toward "by the North gate the wind blew full of sand." Ever since tea leaves covered the tidal reaches of the Charles River whole school of fish take sudden turns from one direction to another. So in the next sentence. Taxonomy, which is ordering par excellence, has eminent aesthetic value whereas taxation has consequences. Two characters of similar meaning, like "face" and "countenance," are often used together as one might open two umbrellas in order to preserve balance. Still, without going into intricacies of cause and effect, the space between two languages is not between mirrors, but curves along the great wall of error, a refined form of adventure.

OTHERWISE SMOOTH

1

How daily my life. How tiny the impurities around which words might accrue. Worlds. Whorls. Pearls? Once I stood in a town where nothing was left unchanged but the clouds driven from the east. Now I learn from the sea. Always the same, always different, brackish body, uncertain. The unusual I hold at bay by taking pictures. To let it accrue to memory without having to experience it? Do we live this way, walking, as if we could, on thin air? But the sycamore stands in the yard all day and all night. And now, though still lifeless in appearance, quickens. Roots gripping farther down.

2

The world rolls away coldly, transposed into vibrations of money. And, like the nerve cells, never comes to rest. No matter how carefully I lime my words. Breath. Faith. Myths. To trap the plumed bird. Tough luck: I look on as it recedes into associations. Experience, *Erfahrung*, contains travel. In German. It happens on the road, and I had put my trust in science to construct one for me. It led to scenic overviews. Then gave out before I could reach, let alone hold, anything fast in my fist. I'm loath to admit: this absence, for all the grist of images, is all I know.

3

Are we never able to touch it? The immediate between the ticks of the watch, the lighthouse flashes, one nerve impulse and the next? Not even with our eyes? A cosmic storm slips between my fingers without the least pressure exerted on the skin. Stream. Thin. Clean. Wind. Only once it's past I latch on. Old light, of dead galaxies. Only once we've said "I" with all that follows do we become aware of pure experience, mute like a newborn's smile. But then it's already over. We console ourselves with knowing the difference, which we call history.

4

If we just sit on a chair we make no mistakes. But starve for contrails, crows, outlines of buds, and strange horizons. Bird flutter. Gunshot echoes. But let's say we worry what is poetry and what is prose. Wonder. Try to know something and incidentally ourselves. Then pain is inflicted. And though it has no form nor special center in the brain it is there. A world closed in itself. Yet wants a voice. Yet whips to the quick the try to stammer it into words. Assuming we were lucky enough to be spoken to before age 12. So that our potential was not jeopardized and now we "have" language.

5

I say "I" and thereby appropriate the entire language. And trust I am, through words, gradually to become. A person? An instance of discourse? Plain as the sky to a fisherman? Beginnings are hazy, below the belt, where a face is not yet possible though already bespoke by gravity. But pronouns do not refer to anything in space and time except the utterance that contains them. Each time, like death, unique. Not like walking in light that lies like fine dust on the ground, but language handing me, each time, the gifts of memory, a past. A soul? While the voice excites intimacies of organic existence, modulates the frequency of pulses from nerve fibers. Code. Clouded sentence. Crowded square emptied of bustle by a sudden rain.

6

It is in grief—a sister's death, a friend's—that I admit: for this I have no name. The words are empty shirts and pants strung on a clothesline. Without body. Without air. Therefore I too can't breathe. Sore. Sere. The self goes from the self. Pain felt as in a twilight state, first stutter of sleep, as on the outer limits of the soul. And even the pain I feel might not be mine. Here they are, sister, friend, dead and tired. From the effort, without the help of language, to stand up in my memory. Which has lost its simple-mindedness, its clear-cut narration. Suddenly old.

7

After the first hour the mourners fall silent. Or speak at angles, in a hush. You have an importance we did not grant you while alive. Now you obstruct the passage of time you're no longer in, and the clocks risk stopping. The rock has split. Early. Eerie. Lack of experience translates into shock. The clarity, the final simplicity of excessive complications. Preoccupied zone in the brain. My face none of the different blacks of mourning, but white and red as always. You would prefer our mourning raw. But I need conventions to lean on. Pomp on circumstance.

8

Without you to say you to. Without you saying you to me. Words don't rise to the roof of the mouth. The rose is obsolete. The color of your eyes subtracted from the air. Fabric undone. A twist of wind. Waste. Dust. The walls crumble to memory rubble. This hour a month ago, a year, your head in the mirror, sun on a leaf, strident chemistry, dashes of cold rain, sentence crashing down. Woodsmoke floating above it all. And a silence I can't bear because it is complete.

9

Grave, tomb, menhir, dolmen, cromlech, cairn, pyramid, coffin, black-box. The earth our mother. Caught in a movement that doesn't seem to take place. With fields enough no end to plain. And bursting with buds. Death gleans no electric charge. No meaning. Only a window slammed shut. I keep circling. One excessive, emphatic quote: no space not crushing, no rain not maddening, no state not a vastation. And yet. Already so many pear trees blossom. Unscroll patches of soft velvet. The hand touches and lingers.

LAMENT

NO BOTH

Michael Gizzi, 1949–2010

Clocks may well run at different speeds in the mountains and in the plain, but your book is called *No Both*. There was a blur of force in your eyes, an arrow shot from too far back to reach its goal. Winter's home in the winter body. So that you were able to save the maple in front of my house, but not yourself from falling. When you had wanted to be a bird.

Just this, you wrote, a note on depression, my own shirttail shortcomings, flayed caul of pain, sharp as Billy Occam's scar collection, and the hearts on your sleeves fray.

You moved fast trying to match your feet to the speed in your head. Enough breath for the rollercoaster through the dictionary, not for that upright recovery of ease with your self. Two words next to each other resonate presence, the happiness of passing from nothing to all, with meaning not given by nature. Unbridled dreams. Naked I, almost indecent.

Expect to rustle an angel, you wrote, holes in socks not fit for history books, the heart is a cliff, we'd prefer not to speak about our feelings.

The anger within your melancholy was a black within the night. Which also falls, attracted to the slow-down near the ground. Bottoms up, the one-way narrative. *Va, pensiero*, in your perfect glottal yodeling, the next-to-nothing vibrato of your body. It's turning cold, the leaves red.

April's hem giving way to mayhem, you wrote, on the high seas (three of them flat) leaves move to reflect a monstrous endowment, magical plenitude, speckled branches.

You joked nonstop, intent on covering up your flayed body with handrails for climbing on level ground. What a struggle, casual relations. Pretending to enjoy our company you opened the sluice gate. Spendthrift words falling on our ears multiplied the present moment, with peculiar motions in the mind, not to forget pleasure. While you stood there, a solitude inhabited by manic song, snowy egrets, private river parts.

Ancient hiccups belly up in mist, you wrote, all the pies of our half-lives, off the streets from yesteryear, millstone in knapsack, my heart's so fired up it's beating on the other side now.

Even a god needs a witness, but a lover's close withness suddenly feels like an error. Gravitational drag. Your ribcage open to the public, you wish for a bit of indifference, neglect. Misgivings huddle in the corner. You want a dead guide to chat with while diving down 50 flights of maple.

With vexation, you wrote, as though straddling a high tension wire, and the wind in the willies, the world is getting smaller, get your ass outta my soul.

In the laws that describe the mechanisms of the world, there is no difference between past and future, cause and effect, memory and hope. There is no present, as there no longer is for you. In *our* present, the bubble around us, it is too late to ask where you lay down in river silt like the stone always beside itself. But your words still gather the light at the horizon. Your dark bird swims overhead.

I hope you're well, you wrote, I am a welt, in Ameranguish: "How do little et tu soon mortu buzz?" please don't think me, I no longer care to appear.

WHITE IS A COLOR

1

Suddenly. Your body makes a cross with the curb. The air stopped,
shutters shut. Though the sky is swift and narrow as a river gets deep.
As the lungs inherit and weather. We'd come to see a play.

2

Flutter of eyelid without sequel. Body vanished into numbers to deter-
mine if you are a body. The taste of gravity stays in your mouth. Stage
empty, even the silence not itself. Though rescue is already on the way.
As if it were possible.

3

A broken vertebra exerts pressure on the spinal cord. Till waves spin
in all directions. Your dead rise from the undertow and drift through
your body. Languorous, without gravity they can't get a grip on creases
in your skin. They slip, blown east to west by the wind. Then there is
nothing to comfort your eye by deceiving it.

4

White has come to stand in for time. Standard, as if an interval could
become permanent. The segments of your life are laid side by side on
the operating table. Skin peeled inside out. Deep strata unreconciled.
I circle the rim, trying to foreshorten it into perspective.

5

Intubated, intrusive, intimate, independent breathing failed. Images do not come this far, or narratives. Today is today. The stage remains inert. An unconformity, I hope, between two periods of brisk. I wait with all my energy for the curtain to rise.

6

Gauze pressed to neck. Vertebrae realigned into forgetting barely interrupt white sheets. You didn't think time could abandon you: stopped motion, without verbs or tenses. You do not move. Not. Not move at all.

7

Apprenticed to the allotted white, but unable to gauge the distance to unthinkable. Only by speculative means, I'm told, can we grasp physical reality. The atmosphere covers you with one hundred forty-four blankets of lead. No longer transparent for rays of light. Loathsome as the world is, said Wyndham Lewis, I like to look at it. Or anything painted in oil on a flat surface.

8

Our bodies have, in millions of generations, learned how to inhale and hearty what the atmosphere metes out. Only your breath catches under water, with your dead. White without recourse. Whereas my emotions tumble ahead in their allegiance to sequence, you can't lean forward. The way a sentence does. Toward development or conclusion.

9

You are suspended the way a mountain floats on an inner layer of the earth plastic enough to behave like a liquid. With weight loss, as rocks loosen and roll down to the sea, you rise. Into what inner self, what unfinished canvas? And breath, with effort, opens. Into sleep. Where a vicious circle threatens to dream you.

10

At night, when the moon is in the south, and gravity sleep-soaked, you ride the constant curvature. Form displaced, eclipse, false star. Westward across the sluggish river, mountains and wide dreary plain. To repossess. The child you were and paint Emporia red. Till world enough comes white to check its level in your blood.

11

My heretofore hot hurry has dissolved behind me. Like a bridge in a fairy tale. I walk different streets, past tulips or flowering Judas, to the same white walls, white face. I tell myself white is a color. Opaque, Runge said in a letter to Goethe, and rarely seen pure. But contains all possible points of view.

12

The shadows of your dead hover by your side. They hold pieces of the puzzle. Keep you from being all that you are. When all waves are the same length the scale thins to the finer calibrations of fantasy. But the body never is, you'd say, all that it is. And it makes no difference.

13

I make random forays. From your gravitational pull. As if there were paths out of orbit. As if not every second were unraveled. As if I were not locked in lost for words. You cling to your bed as if it were the frame you're painted into.

14

No matter how much debris, how hard the repairs, how many walls and slow. I know you want to be here. In the strong air. The space of a word, black against white shall be no more. And will not let go the apples of the earth. Or the beautiful deceptions of the light.

15

Staying still. Then not so still. Then almost moving. If at first there was nothing, even legs that buckle remembering the vertical are something. A single note still haunts the rehearsal. Looking out of a museum window, you say, would be more complete.

16

Uncertainty scatters performance over but, because, what if. The cliff, sheer drop to the sea, reshapes into a mountain. Are you equal to the strain of breathing up these slopes? Back to a world that's red and blue and green? With air, with as much air as parts for whole and ink and paper? And other ambitious undertakings?

17

Of moving you know the slowness that feels like standing still. An eternity to cross from bed to armchair. Lateral freeze. Selves scattered into less than motes in a thin sun. Can you see cherries turning red, throwing your shadow on a lawn, attempting real time? At least you look more like yourself again, and everybody likes resemblance.

18

Recovery: an unfamiliar element you haven't learned to swim in. And would rest where you've not managed well enough to leave alone. Between white cancels all else, window, and water. A phrase unable to find its margin. Are there eventual islands, ships over the horizon? Harbor lights?

19

Fragile, dense, opaque, obstacle, the body. Elusive like the foundations of a theory, even when words are open all the way. A limit to our arts and crafts. Your once upon a watershed, your play about the not forever. Are you now leaning forward to embrace me? Or because you are again about to fall?

IN ANYONE'S LANGUAGE, AGAIN

SILENCE

Your silence which. With a question of punctuation. Seems to repeat. Elsewhere a long complicated life. Syllable by syllable isn't. The slightest pause. What I wanted and. Therefore this curving to tell you.

ERROR

What's called a normal. Life a series how long. Of grainy errors. Irritating if you feel that way. About errors. Rather than be afraid of words or not really. Afraid but a sense on an empty stomach. Of having already said more. Hauled water from. Than was there. Or that a task could. While it happens to you. Circumscribe. The most terrible things happen.

NOUNS

You might grasp at. For safety. A point of view agreeing. Like a verb, having to, with whatever you do. But disturbing nothing. Or in rocky terrain only. When the dark by any other name will hold its ground. Would washing our hands help us also to connect? The scattered fragments of perception? Your refusal, when you talk about winter. To use figurative language. It helps, even if it distracts, to go with nouns. To have that choice. Even bold ones like "love."

ALREADY DISTANCE

Not being able to decide or measure. The space I had given to you. A weakness that could appeal. Drift could do that. To weakness. Work was to be done. With writing, with the endless sentence. A sandy feel to the skin and along with it. Not matching my all thumbs to your thumb. And motes of dust.

PUNCTUATION

Not just a blind pause. As if it had force. Like prepositions, attentive to. In writing that is. To everything except meaning. Or dawn. Taking your hand, or someone else's. Not like a name that's been spilled. More having an interest in facts, or Shakespeare. Though always: the rain.

COMMAS

What had periods of reflection to do with it, or commas. Long curving roads. A sense of sequence. Hoping to come closer, and I don't mean to the single pore. Was howling up the wrong, headed south for trouble, hollow tree. Because I don't want to. Get anywhere. Inward and awkward become formidable power.

INTENTIONS

I can't being heavier now. Attribute. Bad intentions to you. Because pressed. Silent as when sleep comes. You're so totally without. Intentions altogether and unable. To use not drifting either. Though known as cold or. Flat words could. Come to mean disarmed.

DETOUR

The telephone calls, there are too many. So difficult too. All these difficulties to work and work at. Not managing, and you trying to help. In your way. Your discouraging way. But then, to float like this, get used to doubt. You have, or come to, nothing. Not touching, as with a nerve end. For a liquid to turn to ice when everybody. Knows the question is not. The feeling one could have about it. Of strangeness because of how, in minerals. And not wanting. To detour.

THREAD

for Sawako and Eugene

In love, in the wide open, we. Seem to pass through entire worlds. Though steam rises and we know we must. By no means, in even brighter. Light or ever. Let the thread break.

POSSESSIVE CASE

It wouldn't be a push. Toward land. As much as soaring on clipped wingtips. I don't try to reach by loaded dice, by slow light, glacial. And am not surprised, in the possessive case, that there's no land there. Not for me. Though I went at random and therefore. Could not ever hope to stop.

A COUGH

Your name, why go on calling it. Having already. Struggled, it does no good like giving in. To a cough. Or trying to. Always in question mode, leave. An almost labyrinth, the street going on such a very long time, but even. Even bleary and inattentive, I feel. The color of air, resistless.

A word in anyone's language. A sound, translated gesture, an obstacle. Why go on worrying it. A question, which is not a fabric. Fishing for whatever's not a word. Could tell of the instant, you in your chair. The great dreams of the night. The fog I breathe.

THE SKY

I was, had, exhausted. The question. When it is true there is your thin brief voice. And exclamations. But inward where. With an effort of memory, it may look like a garden. But haven't you hurt yourself? By accident? Which, even in an old enough story. As if it could unfold, along the edges. This "V" of Canada geese.

What shall we do. While thinking about it. For such a long. Ashes of
dead stars passed into. Such a very long time that. The book of minerals
too. Too hard to read. Driving, not really fast, but. Wanting to. Take our
distance. From thinking about it. Which is not

YOUR NAME

The question how to open. Your name. Kneedeep or farther and not telling you, not. In that way. A map, even scaled down, would help to know. What I want and what really is. A name. Hugging the body, not breaking the skin. But almost. Preferring a lock on limits. Perhaps an amulet.

THE NEED

Believing it can be met. To talk in the wind, or to. In spite of cold fingers, this need so exhausting. That more. And more than necessary. One does not use nouns. So I ask myself when even the president. Though the weather turned. The trucks heading north. Taking up the road, the trucks. Heading north, whereas writing. Makes it bearable. Grammar so exciting to put together. Or time. Fumbling with. The need to say "I." Half-heartedly. Pronouns can be so mistaken. So without.

YOUR SINGULAR, MY LOVE

Is it what I want? I tried not to tell you, not make you see that I'm opaque to myself. Lost among electrons and protons and neutrons, arms tangled with legs. Precipitate fear that writing, though I'm waiting for it, would make me a shadow. Or are we already? And still not worthy of the dark?

ERASED REFERENT

One must think of, but finally, I had to agree, not walk around naked, not in body or spirit. Not write about, when what is a word, at the risk of disconnection no longer ask. What it would take. Acknowledge the dark, though with dreams in color and. If still possible. Moist skin against the page.

EXCESS OF AIR

And so ask: winter? this winter? Not with writing pressing in. A variety of large and empty, but perhaps only a tone. Whereas winter means already distance, break of energy. Regardless of kisses, snow. Weighing down the branches, not feeling.

CONJUNCTIONS AND CONSTITUENTS

Love, lord of. Such a silly and out loud. To disperse a crowd for a sentence when a tulip is a tulip. Not only in Holland. Tried to approach. But what of the dishevelment and intermittence? I've been living on the verso of. What shall we, or was it joy? Slow says the body across the dream.

LAMENT

Edmond Jabès, 1912–1991

I wanted to write a poem to Edmond Jabès. To call to him across the border of death. And, at the same time, to comfort myself.

I put down phrases like: "a rift in the air," "the grain too much against." Or: "pronoun riddled with holes."

I tried:
> I would call you with so close a name
> as makes the dark
> less deep
>
> . . .
>
> I would line up the blank space
> that is the matter
> between words
> so that a yeast of questions
>
> . . .
>
> I would separate deep
> from structure
> until grammatical movement
> recapitulates
> your slow walk

It did not work. I kept remembering the passages in his work that anticipate his death and felt he had in a strange way preempted my attempts.

The word "preempt" began to preoccupy me. I found: "Latin *prae* = pre- and *emere* = to buy, more at REDEEM."

I saw I had tried to forge a balance of sound and void. Had tried to pre-empty, rather than preempt, the emptiness in order to flip it into its opposite. It could only be flippant. Forged. It could not "buy back."

The only way I can call to Edmond Jabès is with the weight of his own words, impersonating them in a different language. With *what the black of fire carved into the white of fire.*

CUT WITH THE KITCHEN KNIFE

Hannah Höch, *Cut with the Dada Kitchen Knife through the Last Weimar Beer-Belly Cultural Epoch in Germany* (1919). © 2021 Artists Rights Society (ARS), New York / VG Bild-Kunst, Bonn). Photo credit: bpk Bildagentur / Nationalgalerie, Staatliche Museen, Berlin / Jörg P. Anders / Art Resource, NY.

1

Despite dramatic changes in women's status. During the Weimar Republic. Their economic situation did not improve. Hannah Höch was thrown into the sharp indifference of the city. While the eye swivels, endlessly, to recognize the January sun as sun. The artist is concerned with appropriating the dead. The objective immortality of fact. (The way you fish a pickle out of a jar?) Some nights are not as dark as the soul, though the days will become darker. Pictures, pennies, paper. Faith in reason is not a premise: it's an ideal seeking satisfaction. Like freedom, movement, sexual pleasure, Dada, revolution.

2

One must have thoughts cut with the kitchen knife. By Hannah Höch. To see the body dissected into its restless multiplicity. And the world in brittle winter light, high toward the cold. Compare pulled out of school to care for a fourth sibling. With art, later, pulled out of galleries, the artist into lying low. For now her eye follows its own method: vertigo. Indivisible sensations. Wheels, gears, ball bearings. Clouds are massing, and we cannot account for them. By the sea's evaporation. Though we've failed to find any elements that don't conform to general theory.

3

Sight presumes fissure. Just as language. Is elliptical and requires leaps. But few philosophers admit that our ideas are feelings. World War I stops an art student from traveling to Paris, not from Red Cross work or being a Dadaist's lover. Difficult apprenticeships. Rather than a pinhole for objective reproduction of the world: violent juxtaposition. Of metal and flesh. Antagonistic equivalence, kaleidoscopic, centrifugal. Over deposed Kaiser Wilhelm's left shoulder, people. Who have been cold a long time in line. At the employment office.

4

Clips images from print media as a way of seeing form. Montages with a disorienting variety of perspective. Variation in scale, interruption of contours. And rough, visible seams to see closer to touch. This will be called *entartet*. The telephone brims with signals. Breath rises white like fog. Though Raoul Hausmann and Hannah Höch try to embody the New Man and New Woman. The tolerance of flesh gets lost in the old gender roles. With wind sweeping the streets. Windows, wires, tinder. There must be limits to the claim that all elements can be explained.

5

The deep of the world fills the eyes. With tears. Then to see thought there is need. To speak aloud into the ears. Always, in the real world, the brute fact. Hunger, misery, the chill of winter. The sound of boots marching. But who is the dancer who tickles Kaiser Wilhelm's chin? Why is her head replaced? By Hindenburg's? There is dispute if creative ferment will lead to religion, the internal combustion engine, or National Socialism. But our object of veneration is now orgasm.

6

A naked body connects directly. Dada Evenings, Dada Fairs, Dada Exhibitions. Unthinkable some years later. Hannah sees unfettered freedom with one eye larger than the other. As if through Hausmann's monocle. As when the dark upon the face of the deep gave way to forms. Unfurled sky, a bug, arrow, paintbrush, scissors, ball of wool. Philosophy can only introduce us to subject/predicate, substance/quality, particular/ universal. But reality is. Except for the rent. A matter of fine-tuning. An excited condition of the retina.

7

Panic breaks out at the barber shops: German women hold elected office. Nipple, bud, eyelash, comma. They walk a high wire. The men hope, right into the Baltic. And that the wind lift up dresses and show the blindness of flesh. That Hannah's role remain making coffee. Do we still expect space to be homogenous, as seen by an intelligence without body? And that perceiving an actual being objectifies her into data? The fully clothed feeling of satisfaction. Could a bodiless intelligence drive a horseless carriage? Or does satisfaction blanket all additions?

8

It is winter. The pine trees crusted with snow, and the air tense with wires. Hannah's photomontages respond to the shifting representations of the New Woman: dancers, actresses, Marx, Lenin, and other revolutionary figures. In color. Which is itself a degree of darkness and will veer to brown. (Shirts.) What light there is travels in waves. What isn't clear is the sudden turns. A paper airplane takes from one direction to another. Or public opinion. Or that art should embody the adventure of hope.

9

The way Hannah juxtaposes. Athletes' and dancers' bodies with piles of machinery, cogwheels, soldiers. Hooks the pleasure principle to the moment it crashes. Into reality. You'd better look from the corner of your eye. Bank, dime store, orphanage. Or with the eyes at the end of your fingers. Then doubt evaporates so that a complete feeling. In regard to the universe, thinks Hannah. Will bring about a transformation of the heart. In spite of the temperature. And murderous militias.

10

The dominant emotion. In Depression-era Germany was anger. What happens if it couples with the pleasure of nostalgia? A gleam shagged with flags and tending toward violence. The initial fact (anger) is macrocosmic in the sense of being relevant to all occasions. Work, no work, funeral home. The horizon takes on considerable weight, as it does before disasters. And paralyzes our feelings. The view so abstract it might not exist. The words *snow is falling* are spit like a curse. At snow falling. On bicycles and BMWs.

11

In the center, the dancer Niddy Impekoven's body. Kicks montage into motion across the wall between pure art and pop culture. Muskets and watermarks. Why is she decapitated? Anticipating the coming atrocities? Her arms reach for Käthe Kollwitz's head that floats away at a diagonal. Head expressionless except for its name. Which, like Hannah's, will become suspect. The eye sits like a spider at the center of its nerves. Is it true that the final fact is always microscopic? Peculiar to the specific occasion, e.g., leaving Raoul Hausmann? A foreclosure that stirs the heart?

12

It is difficult to know if representation of pleasure will, through desire, motivate change. The body always relevant. An optical stimulus and perhaps lovely. Perspective on clothes and bones. Gustav Fechner damaged his eyesight by staring into the sun in the course of research. On afterimages. A piercing realization that vision is corporeal. Then does it need to refer to the cups and saucers outside it? Sometimes Hannah does a little two-step. While philosophy knows only solitary substances, her world is buzzing with fellow creatures. Unlike some years later. When you don't dare speak to a neighbor.

13

A grid format implied by vertical strips of paper. Disrupted by diagonals. And the eye, unable to stand still for you to look into. Goes out of the frame to open other horizons. Where the speed of light flashes in all directions. Snow has covered. The most normative behavior along with the museums. On a good day, as the eye so the object. At other times Hannah's heart is heavy. Because she feels the approach of jackboots? The subject/predicate habit of thought doesn't admit that facts are in the world like garbage trucks rolling down the street. Or tanks.

14

With high and happy tension Hannah. Makes at least two glossy magazines overflow on the facts. Kaleidoscope gifted with consciousness. She scissors a grand jeté across. Up down right left high low. Escaping from the ordinary she annexes what little hope there still is. (Though the water pipes have frozen and burst.) And reveals the complicity. Of metaphysics and perspective. Each exterior thing is a nexus of occasions whereas no person steps twice. On the same sidewalk. No person, in a few years, escapes suspicion.

15

A utopian light captures. Edges of technology and blots out the defense minister and his Freikorps assassins. River, sluice, wall, poplar. Then reality is passage. From one gigantic montage to another by simple rotation. Space comes and goes as in a movie. And the New Woman unfurls her body from right to left. Inviting even the dead to new life. But time is a component of observation. There is a darkness. That seems to grow deeper. Right before our eyes.

16

No chronicle (of the Weimar years) fails to note. The sensation of speeded-up life and the latest Charlie Chaplin. Machines vibrate in all their parts. Wind from the east passes through windows. And other openings. Streetlights striate the night. Which is large. And hides more knives than condoms. Knowledge is founded on particular things, but there are too many. Rows upon rows of eyeglasses. Not sufficient to reveal the shape of horror.

17

Hannah eyes beerbellies to portray Weimar politicians. Recklessness and wintry trees. A mirror to our thinking and all its deformities. While the word Dada emanates from Einstein's head, clouds lined in black. Already mourn the next generation. Driving all thought indoors, denying external referents. The eye is a better witness than the ear. Especially in daylight when it beholds. Nothing that is not there. When the meaning of "thing" is potential. For process. And fear spreads like the flu across the entire country.

18

So powerful. The flood of images. It could sweep the dark night of the soul to distant galaxies. Hannah signs her name in order. Not to lose it. Among dreary woollens and other afflictions. In spite of actuality being incurably atomic, her eyes. Are panoramic like a frog's. She shivers. Because of winter? Of night and fog? Or because she's told: Be careful what you see?

REHEARSING THE SYMPTOMS

WANTING

Wanting, always, the possibility of this body. Thinking it here. In anxiety. In fear. But wanting to want. The light never to stop.

Caught between wanting and acting. Between language and landscape. Wanting to contain volumes, multitudes. Curves to everywhere. Describing circles of light, flashes of lightning.

Wanting the body visible from head to toe and without secret. A nakedness without debts. Believing it possible. The light as event. Thinking to want to think. As if in response.

Doubting I love while knowing I've wanted to. Thinking to console myself. By describing veins in a block of marble. As if seeing. A reason for seeing.

Fearing to exist without really living. Absence of body within the body. Wanting to be able to suffer. To look at the dark. The mass of night that surrounds. Or is myself.

Thinking of the body. Here, without thinking. Not knowing how to think. Swimming without fatigue. As if without body. In a sea without water. Without end.

THINKING

I don't think I know how to go about it.

I sit at the edge of the water. As if it were the right place for learning to think.

As if it were enough to sway with the current. Or indecision? Stay? Walk away? Give in to the sand dunes fading and falling or a quick push upright? If I can't walk might I yet, like Parkinson's patients, be able to dance?

My brain's incessant activity seems fruitless. It can't be thinking. I put it on paper to encounter it outside myself. An obstacle. A wall with a grain, with pores where I might discover a pattern. Then I'm recalled to my body by legs as if pricked by needles.

How can I think when I can't even see, night falling swiftly, shifting around me like water? Can one look at nothing and hope for help?

Is it a matter of rocking with the dark? Monotonously? But I'm speeding or slowing down the long lane where thinking gets lost in layers of dust, failing precision. Failing to see, to embrace. The gulls circling. The vast empty space. Traffic noise borne in on the wind.

Should I take off my clothes, nudity being power? But would I know my body scattered among memories? Impossible to hold in the mind all at once.

If I let the night invade my eyes, all the way to the horizon? As if it had a body? Might I then see the cause of my not seeing?

It might be a beginning.

DOUBTING

for Aaron Kunin,
who walked among these doubts before

Wanting to doubt as if it were liberating, a spectacular absence of obstacle over vast distances. Enough to make me breathe.

Accepting the cracks in the walls, the tightened silhouette. But do I have to refuse consolations and permanent address surrounding my body?

Comparing the coordinates of knowing, doubting, believing—if two or more theories fit the facts? If the facts dissolve in multiple perspectives?

Will I choose the simplest, the most elegant? Or the one that satisfies secret desires?

If I try to justify my choice without shrinking the field into mere surface erosion and wonder, will doubt fill the whole body? Or will it open into a modulation in what does not exist?

Not that I want to destroy, ironize, or even slam the door. I doubt that it would be useful to know myself.

I doubt that I can escape doubt. That I can finish my work. Or even begin, having only kidded myself that I was working.

I doubt that the bits will fuse into a prism for desire or other forms of feeling.

I don't doubt that I'll die. I doubt, at least if I remain in Providence, there will be good weather for the funeral.

KNOWING

How to be alone, for instance. As on an island. To fold inward (like daisies at night, not as in mechanical dysfunction). As if away from the violence which is the meeting of body and order.

To sit on the beach like a perch for a canary. Or bugs. Or words, in order to imagine. Sun moving through me, air flimmering with heat, the sand black and white, lava negra flowing from the volcano.

(This is not in itself knowing happiness. But very different from mere thinking.)

The island is not one of the Canaries. Which, said Pliny the Elder, are named so because they contain "vast multitudes of dogs." The islands are not named after the canary, but the bird after the islands. The tail does not wag a multitude of dogs.

I often don't know what I'm thinking when I seem to be thinking. But know I can't not think in words. I need words as if they spelled survival, were my only perch in the void. That surrounds and threatens.

Not one of my bodies has been on the Canary archipelago. This makes no difference to the islands, but I know that canaries are native and everywhere. In pine and laurel forests, sand dunes, orchards, copses, parks and gardens. As are dogs.

I know because I've read it. I believe words in encyclopedias.

I stroke them and put salt on their tail whether at sea level or on a mountain. More than anything I fear their leaving my body. Leaving me caught behind the tongue, where I did not know my name and had to howl from deep in the chest. Like a dog that doesn't recognize any smell.

Where time was mislaid, and images turned upside down. Then the sun uncurled the previous climate, and again words alight everywhere. But, though Mount Teide has not erupted since 1909, I tremble even in sleep that they, the words, might again become incomprehensible. As hair standing on end is to a hairless species.

DOING

I often don't know what to do. Or if I want to.

Dawn has long broken while I still drag my feet in the mud inside my head, hope for coffee, make a B-flat moan. To prepare the plunge into action. Or not.

Maybe I want to cast only a passing shadow. Feel like my mother's "Thank God" when she took off her corset.

But I am worried there's something I ought to be doing. Afraid I'll die without having done anything. "Realized" myself, you call it, but wouldn't that just mean limited myself? A cement mixer stuck in one motion, even if it helps build a house?

So I delude myself into thinking I'm doing something when thinking. Or when descending into the night with the cat and dreams of the cat.

You say, no doing without sweat of the face, thorns and thistles, and bringing forth children.

Should I look, instead of worrying about fine distinctions that escape my eyes? Listen, instead of fretting about the size of my ears? But can I cultivate my garden without becoming a cabbage head?

The hand gets ready to write. Could we not call this manual labor? Or a stage in the Great Work of rendering the corporeal cat incorporeal while giving her body to the bodiless word? Even if it's from despairing of my own body?

You say, my writing is so slow it's more like gravitational condensation. Or dust gathering on the cleaning supplies.

It's true I'm dawdling as if I had time to watch the formation of geological layers. Though night already seeps through my brittle bones.

I certainly don't know what to do to end my days "gracefully." But the body dies all through our life, thousands of cells every second.

So everything should be very clear.

COUPLING

I often feel I am a different person depending on whom I am with. As a word in a sentence may be felt to belong first with one word and then with another, and will be different.

At a party I get scattered into so many selves I can't invent enough pseudonyms.

I liked the Rosmarie I was with Keith Waldrop. Therefore I became Rosmarie Waldrop and now stick to one name.

This, I hoped, would help me get hold of myself, hands, feet, hair and all. So I could close my eyes in pleasure at having an identity.

But to be contracted into a single being by another person—how strange. Sure enough, the other selves still hover behind my eyes and mock the flimsy construction.

They abuse their resemblance to words as a lure for your feelings. When I try to dive deep into our moments and forage for love I get caught in a puzzle of which me is speaking. And to which you.

Then I gasp for air, shadowy, a mere residue of echoes. The way words grow dim when there is no meaning coupled to the vocal cords.

Instead of the encounter of two persons along one shared edge, or a play of reflection and opposition of two not quite mirroring halves, we are dealing in multitudes.

Should we not enable them? Every tulip wants an open field. The hills all different shapes, the sky so up and out, why should all our selves be cramped into one single nakedness?

As if, undressed down to our contradictions, we need to scatter them into orbit to go on. To curve outward toward distant stars and other pants.

But though the play of many perspectives is enlarging the boundaries. Though all the bodies, one by one, may be the measure. It is hard to breathe among many smelly armpits.

It seems that two selves can't be put snugly next to one another. As in a drawing of an arrow through two hearts. Neither, it seems, can more than two.

A gap remains. And is its own emotion. And a little sweaty.

ESCAPING ANALOGY

I thought everyone likes a good likeness and cultivated analogies to fill the emptiness within. You cultivated the occipital cortex, in the rear of the brain, which guides attention to the visual world.

You dislike the net of "this reminds me of"s that I let spread to the infinite, though *my* universe has slowed as predicted. And lack of cartilage in my joints acts as a restraint on motion.

You don't mind that analogies make the air transparent for things not in front of our eyes. But that these manifestations of the incorporeal keep you from seeing what you see. Blot out the body. Your mother's, for instance whose both eyes were fixed on the hidden side of the mirror. And whose mind stood apart.

You want to be shattered by the cry of the blue jay, the scent of lilac, want to see, even if it's "Bank of America" lettered on a one-story brick building. Because, you say, reality is always in doubt.

And though you take abstraction for granted and play among symbols, you keep firm hold of your hand. In order to feel it touch the sheet of paper, the pen, to see that your fingers are long and thin, and the nails clean.

You would allow all things their own weight and value, but know that they only appear solid, that the elements keep reverting to metaphor. So when you said, in a moment of distraction, I'm flying by the seat of my pants, you (furtively) checked if they were zipped.

I admit that analogies may settle into an economy of reflex and moreover contradict one another. Still, I enjoy placing their overlappings next to each other, letting the contradictions face outward, as in a game of dominoes.

But now I've seen a pain in your face that isn't like anything else. It has left me shattered because it seems to belong entirely to itself. To have its own dimension. I'm unable to understand, as if trying to hold a mirror to what has no image.

When you try to talk about your pain it's as if you had to speak a foreign language. And the words are forgotten a moment before they are uttered.

In that language you remember all the bookstores you've been in, all the changes of seasons back to your birth. From that distance you tell me you once had a German wife.

My grammar falls short of these horizons. And I don't know if I should tell you. I am that German wife.

MEANING

I pursued meaning till sweat started running down my nose. And my hair matted with migraine. I wondered if it took a particular code or special organ. With exclusive nerve connections.

Gertrude Stein says meaning is tardily. So I pinned my hope on growing older, but time did not provide a clue. It wasted itself in a thousand distractions.

I had sense enough not to ask what *is* meaning—a question known to induce mental cramp. But I still looked for it. As though there were an object corresponding to the noun.

It's not as if I counted on deduction as thinking rather than mere auxiliary. But there is nothing to point to, no particular observation that could serve as runway, so the plane has to start off in thin air. As when Agnes Martin paints a grid, and it looks like innocence.

Also, nothing exists on its own. Wouldn't meaning come with a whole metaphysical system? How could I fit such a thing within my hundred twenty-five pounds even if I wash carefully?

A friend says I have to go back home because meaning is connected to memory, e.g., of milking cows. Another, on the contrary, that origins, even language, have to be left behind. Yet another, that we all inhabit it, but never know.

Once, waiting at a light, I thought I almost felt it. Physically. In the wind, the street, the sunlight glistening on wet leaves, people passing, years, even in the policeman's signaling. A pale, almost subliminal blue dispersed among the molecules of air—all else gone without actually disappearing.

It was beautiful. Enough to refute the theory of relativity. But I hadn't been able to see between the rain.

Instead of holding meaning as if it were my breath, I was simply standing in a wet street. Not an experience to prove that meaning exists. Even if my heart beat as if I had encountered it—or at least a thought.

You say, even if it doesn't exist we must pursue it. It's what makes every day matter, become light and spacious. A continent with links to distant galaxies.

Its elusiveness, you tell me, might register more strongly if I studied clouds. Or a painting called *This Rain*. Or cleaned my house so nothing would stand in the way.

But I'm not after demeaning or dreams born of fatigue. And even my tardy mind has come to suspect that meaning is a vertical pain over the bridge of the nose. Or, like everything metaphysical, inhabits grammar.

Then it's not a matter of finding meaning, but pausing to enjoy its possibility. That is, language, and the more tangible meaning of words. Their use, the way they mesh with our life.

To place them on a page. So that air circulates between them. And thoughts become more than anxiety.

Perhaps this way I can outgrow the craving for big answers? as I did the measles?

TRANSLATING

for Richard Sieburth

There are three stages, says Goethe. The first trots, simple, prosaic. The second parodies the other culture, as if it were the only one. The third clings so close to the source that it is same, not similar. Identical within an otherness.

First stage, you say, admiration; second, envy; third, pleasure in destruction. First, attention, i.e., distress. Second, all thumbs, though opposable. Third, wheel, gunpowder, Camembert.

Translate, the sweet birds sang, and early catch the word.

First came the tower, then confusion of tongues. First, one people, one language, one God. Then, out of the ruins, many forms of life.

Who wants a soul that vibrates but to one single note? A mind that gets excited only once? asked Edmond Jabès. Better translate than never.

If you try to set up a mirror between the languages you'll disappear into it.

First you bend over the text and learn vertigo. You doubt and tear your hair. When you open your sleep to its terror, the poem promises it can attend two weddings.

First you move through mist, echoes, panic in multiple directions. Then the ink blackens. Thought refines its ability to kill.

If you try to get out, each word opens a labyrinth.

You must dissect a disposition of elements as complex as that of nerves and cells. Then, with the carnage, lose yourself in the currents deep inside the body. A night of possibles without surface, fixed positions, without form, and void.

Then you begin to hear: A body feels into breath.

You observe the reshaping with a trace of fear. Will it be "Bottom, thou art translated?" Or, if you are in luck:

Out of its dismemberment, strangely. The poem rises. Celebrating, in all its otherness, its precise bilocation.

LOVING WORDS

I have never felt one with leaves, wind, rain and able to cry. Not one with my surroundings like the California Wintu walking upriver, hills to the west, whom a mosquito bites on his west arm. And who on the way back, hills still to the west, scratches the bite on his east arm.

I've filled my house with many different things. As if to create an ecology to encourage diversity of experience. The way areas with greater numbers of animal and plant species are said also to have a greater number of languages.

Yet I've retreated into the two dimensions of page and *perspective cavalière*. Turned my back on the window in favor of definite articles on perception. Of introversion and subcutaneous shivers.

As if there, within my mind, I could conjugate myself and my desires. When it's clear we need the world and its obstacles in order not to destroy ourselves. And even thinking is the inrush of other voices, like Mary's conceiving through the ear.

I is not my name, is anybody's, promiscuously. Language, which is all difference, proves that you and I are not one. Are, though every sentence hopes for love, each wrapped in our own quilt and alone.

When I clear my throat of words and just watch a blade of grass. The green is too strong to be seen. Open myself to wind ripping the air, cars honking and squealing, the sounds are noise and stop at the left ear.

My mind dissipates into dismal mush. Until I return to the refreshment of verbs, pronouns, conjunctions. And the world returns with the dependence of clauses. My senses are inept without auxiliary words.

It is words let me see what I see, feel what I feel. Even what isn't quite feeling yet, but weeds combed by a stream. Only a tip rising here or there, a reflection, a ripple.

Even if ink is the color of where you are not. If putting one word next to another cannot close the distance. Doesn't even a syllable on the tip of my tongue call you across oil spills and gusting winds?

How could words be mere echo or mirror when they give shape to the air? How could I be deceived in thinking that it is words bring me to myself? And reach out and reach, albeit sideways, through twists of syntax, the strangeness between us?

AGING

We feel we've contracted into very dim, very old white dwarf stars, not yet black holes. Wrinkled, but not quite withered. Dropped out of summer like a stone we watch time fall. With the leaves. Into a deeper color. Wavelengths missing in the reflected light.

The road toward rotting has been so long. We forget where we are going. Like a child, I look amazed at a thistle. Or drink cheap wine and hug my knees. To shorten the shadow? To ward off letting go?

So much body now, to be cared for. What with the arrow, lost cartilage, skeleton within. Memory no longer holds up. A bridge to theory and dreams. Impervious to vertigo. Days are long and too spacious.

Though the sun is a mere eight light-minutes away elderly dust hangs. Over the long sentences I wrote in the last century. Now thoughts in purpose tremor, in lament, in search of. Not being too soon? Going to be? Unconformities separating strata of decay?

You say aimlessness has its virtues. Just as not fully understanding may be required for harmony. And blow your nose. You sing fast falls the eventide, damp on the skin, with bitter wind. And here it is again, the craving for happiness that night induces. Or the day of marriage.

The difference of our bodies makes for different velocities. But gravity is always attractive, and my higher speed. Cannot outrun the inner fright we seem made of. Though I gesticulate broadly. As in a silent movie. Running after the train, waving goodbye.

Distant galaxies are moving away from us. Friends, lovers, family. Even the sky shifts toward red. Where every clearness is only. A more welcoming slope of the night. And I don't remember why I opened the door.

Mouth full of moans, you believe the natural state. Is a body at rest. And close your eyes to the threat of your face disappearing. Without thought or emotion. Into its condition. And I thought I knew you.

Are the complications thinning to a final simplicity? The nearest thing to a straight path in curved space? Clouds of gas slowly collapsing? With only one possible outcome? But unlike a black hole I keep my hair on. As I move toward the unquestionable dark.

This dark, Mrs. Ramsey thinks, is perhaps the core of every self. The deep note of existence the ear finds, but cannot hold on to. Across the vicissitudes of the symphony. Or else this dark could be our shelter in the time of long dominion. And though we are not well suited to the perspectives it opens it is an awesome thing to see. Once you can see it.

ACKNOWLEDGMENTS AND SOURCES

Grateful acknowledgment is made to the editors and publishers of print and online magazines and anthologies in which parts of this book first appeared: *1913, Alienocene, Alligator, Aurochs, Bomb, Caketrain, Caliban, Chicago Review, Colorado Review, Columbia Review, Conjunctions, Datableed, Denver Quarterly, Fence, Fifth Wednesday, Formes Poétiques, Gesture, Golden Handcuffs Review, Hambone, Harper's, How2, Lingo, LIT, Mimeo Mimeo, Molly Bloom, New American Writing, Packington Review, Periodicities: A Journal of Poetry and Poetics, Plume, Poem-A-Day* (Academy of American Poets), *Second Stutter, Seedings, Sentence, Set, The Lifted Brow, The Volta, Van Gogh's Ear; 12 x 12: Conversations in 21st-Century Poetry and Poetics*, ed. Christina Mengert and Joshua Marie Wilkinson (University of Iowa Press, 2009), *The Canary Islands Connection: 60 Contemporary American Poets*, ed. Manuel Brito (Zasterle Press, 2016), *The Dark Would: Anthology of Language Art*, ed. Philip Davenport (Apple Pie Editions, 2013), *The PIP Anthology of World Poetry of the 20th Century, Vol. 10*, ed. Douglas Messerli (Green Integer, 2017), and *En Face & Beieinander: Festschrift for Richard Sieburth*, ed. S. Anderson, P. Fleming, J. Hamilton, and D. Hoffman-Schwartz (2019).

The following sequences have been published as chapbooks: *Velocity But No Location* (Sardines Press, 2011); *Otherwise Smooth* (Above/Ground Press, 2013); *Third Person Singular* (Anomalus Press, 2015); *In Pieces* (O'clock Press, 2015); *Mandarin Primer* (Hook Press, 2015); *White Is a Color* (Guillemot Press, 2017); *Rehearsing the Symptoms* (Rain Taxi, 2019); *In Anyone's Language, Again* in "Dual Poet Readers: Four (hardPressed Poetry, 2019).

"In Anyone's Language, Again" is a reworking and enlarging of "In Anyone's Language" from *Love, Like Pronouns* (Omnidawn, 2003).

SOURCES: F. W. Baller, *A Mandarin Primer* (China Inland Mission and Presbyterian Mission Press, 1911); Emmanuel Fournier, *croire devoir penser* (Editions de l'éclat, 1996); Stephen W. Hawking, *A Brief History of Time* (Bantam Dell Publishing Group, 1988); Henry Hobhouse, *Seeds of Change: Six Plants that Transformed Mankind* (Sidgwick & Jackson, 1985); Maud Lavin, *Cut with the Kitchen Knife: The Weimar Photomontages of Hannah Höch* (Yale University Press, 1993); Stephen Toulmin and June Goodfield, *The Discovery of Time* (University of Chicago Press, 1982); Alfred N. Whitehead, *Process and Reality* (The Macmillan Company, 1929); G. J. Whitrow, *The Natural Philosophy of Time* (Oxford University Press, 1980); G. J. Whitrow, *Time in History: Views of Time from Prehistory to the Present Day* (Oxford University Press, 1988); J. Z. Young, *Programs of the Brain* (Oxford University Press, 1978).

The poems also contain phrases from Giorgio Agamben, Anne-Marie Albiach, Mei-mei Berssenbrugge, Maurice Blanchot, Marie-Louise Chapelle, Robert Creeley, Suzanne Doppelt, Craig Dworkin, Michael Gizzi, Barbara Guest, Lyn Hejinian, Yoel Hoffmann, Edmond Jabès, Franz Kafka, Janet Kauffman, Juliana Leslie, Clarice Lispector, Denise Riley, Bruno Schulz, Rebecca Solnit, Gertrude Stein, Wallace Stevens, Paul Valéry, William Carlos Williams, Elizabeth Willis, and Ludwig Wittgenstein.

ROSMARIE WALDROP, born in Germany in 1935, is the author of several books of poetry, fiction, and essays and the translator of the work of Edmond Jabès, Jacques Roubaud, and Friederike Mayröcker, among many others. Her most recent books include *Gap Gardening: Selected Poems* (winner of the L.A. Times Book Prize in Poetry), *Driven to Abstraction*, and *Curves to the Apple*. She is a member of the American Academy of Arts and Letters and was honored by the French government as a Chevalier of the Order of Arts and Letters. For fifty-six years, she and her husband Keith Waldrop ran one of the country's most vibrant experimental poetry presses, Burning Deck, in Providence, Rhode Island.